The Kingdom of Possibilities

The Kingdom of Possibilities

by Tim Mayo

Mayapple Press 2009

Published by   MAYAPPLE PRESS
408 N. Lincoln St.
Bay City, MI 48708
www.mayapplepress.com

ISBN 978-0932412-76-8

ACKNOWLEDGMENTS

Atlanta Review: The Third Little Pig and *Flamants Roses*; *Arbutus*: The Loneliness of Dogs; *Avatar Review*: Blackberry Poems; *The Equinox*: The Wild Boy of *Aveyron*, The Third Little Pig and Partridge Hunting in an Old Orchard; *Four Corners*: The Journey Begins With the First Step; *The Rose and Thorn*: Confession to the Dark Lady and The Obituaries; *Poet Lore*: Retribution, The Frog and the Snake and Father Poem; *The Chrysalis Reader*: Head to Head (under the title Visiting My Friend); *Five A.M.*: Elegy to Socks; *Del Sol Review*: Thumbness (a slightly different version); *Mannequin Envy*: Portulaca, Red Convertible, At a Walmart in Southern New Hampshire, How It Comes to You, About Beauty With a Capital *B*, Naming the Emotions and A Reflective Voice (under the title A Translucent Voice); *Cold River Review*: Mot Juste and The Fisherman on the Screen; *Babel Fruit*: The Confessional Poet's Confession, The Flea, The Ratio of Danger to Love and You; *Inertia Magazine*: The German Doctor; *WinningWriters.com*: The Counterfeit Seal (finalist for the 2007 War Poetry contest); *The Writer's Almanac*: All the Women I Almost Married. Both *Flamants Roses* and The Third Little Pig won an International Merit Award from *Atlanta Review*. *Flamants Roses* has been reprinted in *The Best of Write Action*, and *Liaisons II: The R.D. Lawrence Commemorative Anthology*, and The Third Little Pig has been reprinted in *The Bennington Review*. Two Mothers will appear in *TWENTY-FOUR SEVEN: A Caregiving Anthology*. A number of the poems in this book have also appeared in a chapbook *The Loneliness of Dogs* (Pudding House Publications).

I am grateful to the Vermont Studio Center and their Vermont Artists and Writers Week program. I would also like to thank April Bernard, Henri Cole, Ed Ochester and Liam Rector for their instruction and help with many of these poems. Also Christine Anderes, Sara Barker, Pam Bernard, Susan Clancy-Bowne, Patricia Fargnoli, Patrick Heller, Douglas Korb, John Lerch, Regina Luersen, Jone Messmer, Mark Peterson, Louise Rader, Charles Rogers, Jeremy Voigt, and lastly, Amelia X. for their support and thoughtful comments. Not to mention Ethelbert Miller for his advice against certain titles, and whose support, friendship and kindness are unsurpassed.

Finally, I owe a very special thanks to Martha Ramsey who helped shape the first incarnation of this manuscript and to Molly Peacock who edited one of the last incarnations and lastly, to Judith Kerman and Amee Schmidt of Mayapple Press for making this publication possible.

Cover photo by Amy White. Painting on bench "Les Oeufs" ("The Eggs") is by Andrée G. Naudé. Cover designed by Judith Kerman. Book designed and typeset by Amee Schmidt with text and titles in Adobe Caslon Pro. Author photo courtesy of Amelia X.

Contents

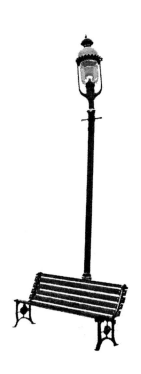

How It Comes to You

It happens waiting for a bus: you cough
under a street lamp, the ground shudders,
steam rises from a grate, and suddenly,
a shabby man thrusts out his hand.

He offers you something small,
purpled like a bruise and oily
as a rubbed jewel in the gloom.
Here, he winces and pleads.

You clear your throat to answer.
All you've wanted is a way to get
from here to there—preferably
the express, but now, a local
has come, and if you turn and leave,
you may never get there in time.

About Beauty With a Capital *B*

About beauty with a capital *B*,
a poem of modest consequence
quotes a Zen (capital *Z*)
story about two monks.

They come to a river bank
where a beautiful lady,
unable to cross,
weeps over her plight.

Not even hesitating, the older
monk carries her across
(A real Samaritan with a capital *S*),
and the memory of her buttocks
never even weighs upon his shoulders.

But having perhaps missed
his last worldly opportunity,
the younger monk gets all hung up
over the forbidden gesture made
by his master. (This is the little *k*,
hard to crack, kernel of this koan.)

The story is famous, but not for showing
how behind each perception of beauty hides
a sensual nut squirreled deep inside you.
How it lies in wait like an apple in your tree.

The lady never thanks her Samaritan,
nor does she eye the younger monk
over the older's frail shoulder

even though she must have felt
his sharp desire piercing
through his master's body
trying to jolt her heart and loins
into his wishful communion.

The poem continues, but being
no longer important to this poem,
the monks go on to oblivion,
because they are Zen,
and the master has already forgotten what
the apprentice will take a lifetime to forget.

And the poet leaves the lady, alone
on the indifferent river's far bank,
weeping because she's beautiful
and beauty is a thankless calling
which, like the river, must constantly
be crossed again and again and again.

The Beautiful Woman

You stare at the jagged tic-tac-toe of her scars
where once a downy peach fuzz grew, and you realize
how beauty is an emotion from which desire splurges
like a prodigal. How it often burgeons, a sudden flower
from a dark and unexpected place where you believed
nothing grew.

                         But here . . . now . . . the livid white knots
of her skin seem to muscle into purple before your eyes
all of that past pain which, to you, is only the discomfort
of what you see and the embarrassment of being caught
as you imagine the indignities she suffered for each mark.

So you glance up at her face hoping she hasn't noticed how
the un-erasable remnants of her past have kept you transfixed.
You look into those eyes, dreading the wise, sad look back,
the dismissal of it all that will scar *you, too*, possibly for life.

The Story You Never Read

One of the small headlines you read tells
how a man who fell from a plane lived,
because a farmer had stacked his hay.

This is one of the stories that doesn't change
the world. History still chugs on like a train
steaming to a station beyond the horizon,
but you get off long before.

So you never read the one about the poet
who died from pushing a pencil, piercing
the drum of his ear to touch, indelibly,
that small, delicate place in the brain

where perception and living converged
then went blank like a new page.

Blackberry Poems

Consider a small canon of them: all plump with their
fruity possibilities, the absent underlying bitterness
to the sweet taste they sing and the inevitable accusatory
stain always found somewhere on a body part; how
the instrumental birds and bees are never present,
though an undercurrent sweeps through the words,
and the prickers always seem to stand at attention
guarding against the poet's hunger. How everything,
which hints of the lush, seems deliciously forbidden.

Now consider the blackberry seed, itself, and
the long heated afternoon you will spend, and on,
into the dark juice of evening and night, prying at
the wedged pressure of the seed exerting itself
between the ivories of your smile, then consider
how you could carry in your mouth the very kernel
of that discomfort, mulling it over like a pearl, but
still leave it out of your one addition to that canon—this
one little seed that makes the blackberry *blackberry*.

The Frog and the Snake

When I was young I came to a garden pool
and watched a snake swallow a frog.

I have meditated long on this
not wishing to leap to the freedom
of just any conclusion as the frog
must have wanted to do,
                              how I saw death's
turbulence reach out touching many around me:
teachers and a woman who pretended to be
my mother, and then not long after the snake
swallowed its prey, my own mother also died.

What I know now was, when she did, I felt
nothing more than I felt watching that frog
move into the mouth of another world,
the marvelous drama of flesh mouthing flesh
and before that, the frog's immobile wish
to be invisible while the snake flickered about
searching.

            How the frog must have struggled
more than my mother did
when she picked up the pistol by her bed
handling it with that casualness in her loose wrists
that comes from drinking too much, and then . . .
the bang.

            It was all over faster than the frog
who had a good half hour to contemplate
as first one leg disappeared, then the other,
until finally his head, eyes bugging impatiently,
backed down the serpent's mouth into the belly
of its transforming future as if bowing
after a long and well played performance.

What I want to confess, though you cannot see,
is that I blinded myself and wandered about
the kingdom of my possibilities for many years.

Waltzing Through

Compare an incident to a small pearl-handled pistol,
its silvered metal embellished with scrolls.
You try to figure what triggers it and how to load
Or disarm it, flicking the bitter pills out of its clip.

Life is full of small, dangerous things.
They are always beautiful. Avoid them.

But do not slink around them, the language
of your bones transmitting trepidation.
Instead, let each muscle and vein carry
the throbbing knowledge of what the brain
cannot hold, reaches for without hands.

Then add to this the little beings of the body:
your corpuscles ticking invisibly together in time
(*one—two—three, one—two—three*) . . . listen.

The Last Gift

People tell me I'm one of a kind—I mean
how many poets do you know who've donned
the ineluctable mantle of the eternal present?

You may ask how I know this as well
as you know the sky is blue, the moon
not cheese, and how a thing called *past*
differs from all that is unknown.

                       To me
only the here and now flickers like a butterfly
before my eyes, but every day, *they* remind me
how I was told yesterday that I will always
have this opportunity—this gift not to remember,
beyond this moment, that which blesses me
with the fleeting present and the ability to erase
all history from a face.

                    Now, I let the turns
of phrase I write come from this special view
that knows no person so each new face
(and they are all new) becomes an Everyman
or woman.

                  Brothers, sisters, and all those
little curiosities which resemble them
with shorter arms and smaller stature
are strangers I have known my whole life,
but only now discover them for who they are.

And only now do these brief words possess
me like this brittle red of autumn I see
as it turns outside my window
falling into the brown past of my future.

Two Mothers

Deep in the here and now, my friend cares
for two mothers. The first resides in a cave
where swallows swoop before her eyes unnoticed
in the dusky moments that are her days.
Evenings, they sing to her in couplets
like blind old bards plucking at their lyres,
and mornings find their shadows flickering
in her head like a far storm.

                      The second lives
beneath a sky where the sun stares down like a stern
eye, and in its light the cloudy skeins of her life
unravel into mad blossoms. All day she hears
the different songs of her daughter twitter
like confused birds above the violent flowers
of her thoughts. Then at night, she spoons her
husband back into the last, small piece of her cup,
and lets the moon spill its soft foam over the one
thin blanket of her sleep.

                      I hear you asking, *Why
does your friend have two mothers?* It is simple.
One lives in the distance where all mothers are,
kept beyond arm's length for your whole life
in a notion whose coffin you will have to close.

The other lives nearer than perfection, but blind
to the world's plumage, she cannot see the difference
between a daughter's flutter and a bird's quick flight.
Nor does she imagine the imperfections of a daughter
she has never had as she listens to my friend start to recite
all the poems that ever touched them both, one by one,
trying to say them all before this mother turns slowly
to the wall and the bone-twigs of her own empty nest.

Father Poem

By now he must be dead, this sower
of a seed that is me, traveling salesman
who humped the farmer's daughter,
soldier, sailor, button on my shoe,
off-rhyme in a couplet I never write.

And if he's not ... what would I say—
as I climbed up feigning the casual,
my thumbs hooked into my suspenders,
up onto the covered porch of the house
where he's been hiding out my whole life,

where he sits in a rocker whittling away
his old age or squinting at an obscure
memory on the far horizon, trying to see it
before the sun sets or the sky clouds up
and everything he's ever remembered disap–

pears—what would I say? How it's rained
heavier than usual these last sixty years?

The Big Picture

Because spring has, at last, dropped its green
over this sparse and tawny interim,

here, at the big picture window we see
the golfers begin to come and go.
It is the third tee, and today two men stop
as if in a layover on a long pilgrimage.
They sit and smoke, then draw gleaming straws
out of a large heavy bag as if deciding
who goes next, though I think I know.

Then after swinging, in a graceful twisting way,
that is a secret to you and me, the first makes
a ball shoot forth and disappear over the rise
and then leans against his chosen stick
and looks on until, nodding, he moves after it
on out of sight while the other struggles
to follow, burdened by a bagful of possibilities,

his companion's fate slung over his shoulder
like a quiver of lead.

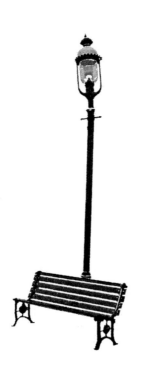

Mot Juste

If it all could boil down to one word,

the distillation of time, objects and your body:

clocks—cars, fingers—noses, lips and limbs—

—everything splaying in all directions—

if it all could only boil . . .

                                   then suddenly . . .
in the long, long story with its shaggy ending

you could shrink the ongoing ribbon of your narrative
and snip it neatly at its end—
                                  right where the evaporable
spirit of what you have struggled to articulate
                                       hardens
like consonants around the illusive vowels
of your life—and you would suddenly . . . *say it*

as if spitting out the little pit of some huge fruit
whose rose flesh inside the heavy green of its husk
had seemed too much for your mouth—until now . . .

Partridge Hunting in an Old Orchard

For Ed Ochester

Day had slumped plumply into sun,
apples fermented on the bough,
and I was logy with it all:

the gold-orange richness of leaves
imbibing the afternoon light,
the sentimental scene I was in

of autumn things in the autumn,
when suddenly my friend shifted,
twisting his body, and fired twice.

I saw two wings rise from a tree
and move away. Then, all at once,
they turned and circled back—all I

had was an upward twitch in time,
faith in someone who knew the woods
better than I—and I shot straight up—

arching back toward what I'd passed,
the whole baggage of my life gathering
in the wake of still air behind me,

and I turned to see the bird's wings fold,
its body fall factual and black.

Nineteen Forty-Five

There are these questions which rise and ebb
like the tides on their twice-daily basis, in and out, up and down,
but much farther apart like blue moons pulling at me.

They have to do with the moment of my conception
and the deluge of its aftermath,
the genetic bean that Jack looks at
and asks, "What does it mean?
Who is this Giant I will meet?"

Somewhere, on an iron bed in a run-down rooming house,
dusk dimming the room like a dying light bulb, and the war
blinking and sputtering, a distant storm in the outside sky,
a man and a woman untwist from the bedclothes
gasping for something the humid air can not surrender.

They are the strangers I have wanted to know my whole life,
whose faces rise like fish beneath the surface. They are
the beanstalk I descend from the present to a past
I will never know:
War has heightened their sense of mortality
to the point that each reached out to the other
to forget the fear of loneliness death fosters.

Outside, you can hear the ocean in the distance,
the lazy slap of low tide on the hard beach,
too spent to regain its height,
and they know there is no future—except
that something (now writing on this page) sperms
and squiggles in her belly: an absence
of planning that passion begets,
the one egg in the basket,
the bad bet that has yet to pay,

and this one poem I write to them, now,
before I toss them, once again, from my mind
never asking that which is too late to answer.

Souvenir (1959)

Once, in *St. Jean de Luz*, village of summer
and light, beaches and bobbing fishing boats,
where the Basques always danced past midnight,
I was young, fresh out of military school, and
each morning splurged into day like a fistful
of coins I couldn't hold. I stood on a cliff
looking at the ocean, the harbor—all the rippling
reflections of sun on the water glinting
like little brass buckles I didn't have to shine.

I watched as workmen, too tired to complain,
filed by like heavy ants. They carried
away dark pieces of things from the earth,
from the deep bunkers the Germans had dug,
and I found my hand reaching for a dirt
crusted strip of metal enlacing metal
in a reminiscent weave that I knew
from all my brief facsimiles at battle
to be an ammo belt.

           So I slipped it
into my pocket. Then, I saw something else
nosing its coned potency up through the earth,
its history buried before my birth,
and I reached down, when, nearby,
a giant ant suddenly rose and spun,
the hairy whips of its antennae waving
back and forth over the object I was
about to touch—the little man shouting out
fierce admonitions to my dumbness.

His face was sad as he took it away
cradling it in both hands—each of them
puckering with scabs, his blunt knuckles white
and red with scars where fingers should have been.
I didn't count what wasn't there, looking
quickly away, as he muttered a curse
that, at first, I thought I understood—though
now, I know I didn't, and though I'm old
enough to imagine . . . I don't . . . I just don't.

Sleight of Hand

For Charles Rogers

Deep in the curling shadows under the spiral stairs
leading to the heavenly bliss of bedrooms above
where my adoptive mother, brother and sister all slept,
deep in those shadows my mother placed her gold
Buddha—not knowing where else to put him.

For years he sat there, cross legged on his oval dais,
gold leaf peeling from his ancient wooden body,
and each day as I climbed the stairs to visit my mother
from my small room behind the kitchen, I would pass by,
fearing the tarnished ghostliness of his presence.

My mother called him the Buddha of Good Fortune,
showing me with her own hands how the two circles
he formed with his fingers came together to make
the sign of good fortune, implying my own.

                                        But I
looked at her hands, the two rings her thumbs and
forefingers made, each one circling its own small part
of earthly emptiness, and I was puzzled by how this
could come to mean what she claimed, and I kept
returning to the Buddha as if he held the answer.

Today, as I tell you this story of hands and fingers
and how, one day, I awoke and the Buddha was gone,
I recall, now, how the rest of his fingers opened like wings
so that his hands seemed to form two birds kissing in flight,
how that might have shown me that the pure luck of being
was as attainable as the coming together of hands.

Flamants Roses

They are more graceful in thought and name
with beaks as big as their heads
and necks that slacken like ropes
from all the weight of their crustacean bills.

Talk has it, in the *Camargue* the winter before we came,
their little brains froze, never thinking to lift their feet
as the circling tides hardened like shackles about their legs.

Men came with hammers and chisels
to chip free their feet, ducking like bulls
the furious black and scarlet sweeps
of their matador wings.
                              Rose flames, they could not
melt nor dance themselves free, their gawky beaks
clacking, scratching the ice like useless castanets.

The Counterfeit Seal

(1968)

In Athens each Sunday of our honeymoon
my first wife and I scoured the old flea market
at the edge of the *Plaka*, beside the ancient *Agora*
said to be the true birthplace of democracy.

We were each searching for that one treasure
whose value dealers of trinkets, junk and
all other items that end unnoticed in life
would not know, but we, in our self esteem
and with countless degrees of ignorance,
somehow would. Everything was so cheap
that we felt we could squander our hearts
and never touch the blood reserves of our love.

But I digress, for it was there I found this seal
of a warrior saying farewell to his wife.
The fine detail of his muscled calf as he turned
from his spear, shifting his concern to his wife's
imploring arms, made me think I'd found mine.

I didn't know then that an art of significance
was what I was searching for, nor did I see
the true meaning in his implied turning back.
None of this was etched into that piece
of colored glass as I saw the sun flash through it
highlighting each muscle of his readiness to leave
for something he deemed more important than love.

The German Doctor

We spoke in French, the Doctor and I.
His first words were to apologize.
To say they had found him guilty.
He had spent three years in prison.

Il y avait des expériences, experiments,
he said, ordered by his superiors.
Qu'est-ce qu'on pouvait faire?
What could he do? I had no answer.

—Nor did I ask for the particulars
of what he'd done. After all, it was
our first night, a cocktail ice breaker,
on a Mediterranean cruise, and only now

do I imagine, forty years later, the splaying
open of skin, the meticulous peeling back
of its layers to shade a lamp in the quiet
leisure of my living room: slippers, pipe,

my well worn leather chair, its own skin now
crackling with age, and that good book I am
more than halfway through as I anticipate
the comforting justice of its ending.

Retribution

It's as though you've grown a third hand.
Out of your elbow, it shoots straight back
pointing to where you've been; you start
to go through life backwards, shaking hands,
making peace with everyone you've left behind,

and you tear up all the insults you've handed out
like calling cards the color of teeth.
You raise your hand and throw them to the wind:
they flutter off awkward as fledgelings.

People compliment you on this gesture,
even though you can't really face them,
and you feel nothing is quite how you want it,
that, somehow, nature has conspired against you:
twisting your bones to make your body humble.

The Loneliness of Dogs

About spelling the human masters
were never wrong, making me wonder
at what age did their cleverness reveal
that god spelled backwards was dog?
Later in their lives, a larger orthography
came to define them in their own letters:
somewhere between animal and angel.

But for me it's always been a dog's life.
And if a deity ever entered my shaggy
existence, it was only the unlettered moon
to whom I howled all those nights
when a restless emptiness slipped
over my fur like a black glove,

and I became the hand that fed me.

The Wild Boy of *Aveyron*

(Paris, 1801)

I named him Victor to vanquish the animal in him.
I tried to teach him to name his own needs,
to have his words rise up from the core
of his body, ball up in his throat, then push out
in well formed vowels quelling the inarticulate.

But all he could gargle out was the word *lait*
as if somewhere between tongue and throat
the muscles that made his words had lost their way.

Lait became his insistent call for love
and the angry expression to all the words
neither my little briberies of milk nor
my *punitions* could ever make him say.

Later, I tired and returned to Paris,
but sometimes, in the dark *non sequitur*
of night, when dreams should take me away,
Victor comes and shakes me. I watch him
press his nose against the window,
confused by its impenetrable glass,

and I see the moon's milk-glow fracture
down upon his face and the hills, caged
between the mullions, huddling outside.

Then grinning with a feral joy, he pulls
again at my sleeve saying his one word
over and over, until he turns back, and tilting
his head up, he opens his mouth wide and waits
for the moon to pour in . . . and I fall asleep.

Name

When I was told my name wasn't my name,
the father and mother faces in my life
each took on a new countenance,
and something ripped apart inside
like a coat suddenly too small.

My size of self changed; body
and soul unplugged; the one slipped
from the socket of the other, and
the arc between them sputtered silent.

The face in the looking glass
took on a distant familiarity:
someone to whom each day
I offered my razored hand.

Falling Off in Another Country

When you fall from the *mobylette*
at the curve in the hill where the straight road
suddenly dips into its soft shoulder,
and your hand rips open to the bone,
breaking your fall, you go to the farmhouse
lived in by the Italians come to harvest
the fruit you, too, have come to harvest.

No one speaks a common language,
but gestures show your wound.
They seat you, surround you like a bandage,
open the medicinal wine for you to drink,
and they clean the pain from your hand,
trying to rub the dirt from your bone.

You leave drunk. Your hand will crust
and scab for weeks. Meeting strangers
will remain painful and, even now you still
wince when you shake hands, wondering
how to let go of the hand that led you here
the one that twisted you to a full throttle.

Finally, a day comes like all the others,
you look down, and the deep stigma
welting in your palm has disappeared,
and just like that, you've fallen off the past
you can never climb back to undo:
the wound, the wine, the ugly, bare
bone of yourself that you once saw.

I, Lazarus,

Actually, I didn't remember a damned thing.
Not even that welcoming light at the end of a tunnel
which others before me had alleged, how it gave you
a severe case of the *warm-and-fuzzies* and renewed your
faith in another place.
                  But I had to make up something
to tell all those who reached out to touch me, their eyes
starry with tears and wonder, their dirt-caked hands
trembling under the influence of resurrection.

                        So I
described how the flesh had fallen from my bones,
each muscle, tendon and piece of fat melting away,
how then I'd heard the clatter of my walk down a cold
dark corridor until that sudden invisible voice lifted me
up from the darkness and the earth around my bones
returned to flesh.
                  It was the least I could do, but once
returned, I couldn't help but touch everyone back,
even fingering their privates, claiming the blessing of life
was the body as they turned away suddenly askant.

The Obituaries

Each day the page would fill with loss,
and he would see the print squirm
through his glasses like a virus
he recognized but hadn't caught.

His wife began to read them, too,
not long after they were married,
but when they stopped for that same
no reason they'd first read them,

something small had already found
its slot between their bodies, and they
warmed it, though it remained thin
and pale as a page waiting for its print.

Finally, a fine print appeared,
and the page thickened into pages,
became a tome wedged between them
which they kept but never read.

Aiming Offhand for a Head Shot

When I fired, the doe just dropped from sight:
no leap upward or backward from the push
of my bullet, no dramatic stagger, no acrobatic
dance I imagined death would always have us do—
just a stumble as if her legs had suddenly lost
their memory, why they stood there, and what
they were supposed to do when not standing.

But she fell too fast into that invisibling
space a windfall makes in the ground, and her
sudden absence made me doubt I'd
ever seen her—and if that—why not myself?
So, I searched reaching out through memory's
veil, past the distance between hunter and prey,
to a distance between mother and son, and there,

for a birthright to my being. When I found her,
I looked down at the empty space above her neck
trying to find a definition of what I'd aimed for,
but all that was left was an eye clinging by one,
last strand of veined ganglion to her earth
entangled body, and that eye could not look back,
could tell me nothing of what I looked for.

The Ratio of Danger to Love

Once, I walked the tightrope
of a round guard rail on a bridge
carrying an injured woman to safety.

Below, cars sped impatiently
across the long macadam reach to home
not knowing that above, on a stretched
tube of stainless steel,
                             a new Wallenda
was trying out his act: balancing
on his hip a frightened woman all jelloed
into incomprehensible gibberish
claiming she had finally seen the light
as her car rolled roof over wheels
into the chaos of the breakable.

And I was complete.

The Word in the Story

It's so hard to tell the story you're in,
not the one that happened yesterday,
but today's tale where your embellishments
of sky, sun and earth—even the clouds—divert you,
and all the people turning about you go
in directions they alone seem to know.

It's what it all means that escapes like the air
in the palm of your hand as your fist
tightens about the present—that same fist
which has held the past by the throat
shaking it for all it was worth until you felt
a gasp coughing up through its craw
to vowel into the air and form that one word
you understood and wanted so much to hear.

You

We were walking on the beach,
someone and I.
I want to say you,
but I am still weighing the small ghosts of our actions.

It was night and the world
was so obviously cold,
a cold calm
that comes from being outside a bar
instead of in.

A woman staggered out,
and for a moment, the stars jangled
with a honky-tonk sound

then settled back to look down.

Teetering out toward the water
over the soft indifference of the sand,
she suddenly turned back to face
the empty road and the closed door of the bar
and, with a swift hike of coat and skirt,
dropped her undies, squatting down to pee.

She hadn't seen us
(we were like the witnessing stars—but closer
and on the same level as the rest of the world).

And there, in the untinseled dark,
the small waves slapping away
the jolly voices of *Jingle Bells*,

I was seized with the sudden desire

to-run-the-hundred-yards-of-beach-toward-the-curling-crescent-
moons-of-her-hips-and-take-her-swiftly-from-behind-pressing-
myself-into-that-soft-side-of-*her*-self-which-she-couldn't-see . . .

then I wanted a wind

to whip up the sand around us,
cloaking us in a Biblical manner,
the air mingling with fire and the fine grit of stone,
until we would both be charioted away
to that place we all imagine.

Instead, my companion
commented on the form of her squat,
grading her like an Olympian of failed attempts,
and we laughed.

This is something you wouldn't have done,
which tells me, now, it wasn't you
but some ghost I will never be rid of.

Confession to the Dark Lady

To A.

Now I am an old man touching desire
like the *nombril* of my body,
picking lint out of its center,
folding myself to sleep like a towel.
I dream of your lips red as welts
against your white face, and I cannot
imagine your teeth, because the redness
of my dream blooms so vermillion—
but you must have smiled at me, once,
making the measured grimace of my face
relax its muscles, letting something,
hard as a pearl, go limp in my brain.

The Confessional Poet's Confession

Now I see I lacked imagination
writing so many poems in that same person
until the *I* of my typewriter wore out,
and *I* was banished from the page
guilty of nothing more than my own experience,

that consciousness I never stepped out of
to enter the head and see through the eyes of another—
say, the woman I once lived with and loved.

Today the hormonal tides of her absence start
to rush through my veins, and I suddenly feel
the full flood of her presence rising so fast
that, soon I'll be over my head drowning
in all she should have held against my capital *I*,

that way I saw the world, where the blinders of my being
cropped off her existence at the knees
so she had nothing to stand on
while the unshakable earth
affirmed itself beneath my feet.

The Little Pet Peeve of Truth

It hangs around your story and mine
saying something different about the same
event. I gather it up for each word I write
like a flag that shouldn't touch the ground.

But in other stories, you wipe the grime
from its snout and send it back to a low place
for more—like the ferret it loves to be.

On it goes, down a hole we never saw before,
further and further through dim tunnels
until it finds a familiar heart-shaped room.

Still, it always comes back to the hands
that feed it for those last few crumbs
we must turn out our pockets to give.

Head to Head

She sees me hesitate to pet
her horse.

       The horse necks her head
further out of her stall. My friend says,
Put your forehead up against hers,
and I lean forward closing my eyes.

We stand there in silence,
the horse and I, bending to reach
each other, the rough brown hairs
between her eyes scratching the pale
winter-patina of my brow.

I can smell horse as intimately
as I could my friend years ago.

Outside, the Equinox shifts
its silent hands in the air,

but we continue, *tête-à-tête,*
until we both seem to know
when to separate, to shuffle
away toward straw and small talk.

Now your horse knows more about me
than you do . . .

       My friend shrugs,
looking away as we walk
out of the barn into the same
old repetition of Spring.

The Flea

I keep reading tales of transformation
in which a human abstraction adds
symbolism to an otherwise mute beast.
In one, epistemology becomes a flea,
making the flea's mind bigger than its body,
grounding it with sheer knowledge, wingless
against its own inescapable brilliance.

What does it mean to be immensely endowed
with a notion of knowledge that encompasses
knowledge itself? To possess it all in a skull
a hundred times smaller than a thimble—its
weight making your brain bow? Where does
the flea put down such a burden, lay its hairy
leg against the prickly succor of its mate?

How can it ever take pleasure again
in the horny rub-a-dub-dub of another
when it has already entertained
all the possible thoughts of its lover
and known the quick twitch and hop of its
mate's hesitation before it happens?

Self Portrait in a Drawing Class

For Amelia X.

Once again, I've entered into commerce with myself.
I have chosen to lift my writing hand to make these lines
express the parentheses of age forming around the unim-
portance of my mouth as if telling me all that I've written
holds no sway here.

                      I notice the slight bend in my nose
which reflects the brick wall I met one night in an alley
after too much drink had led my mouth to say those
unimportant things someone else had thought important.

But it's the heavy lids of my eyes that surprise me.
Suddenly, I see a weight I must have been carrying
my whole life beginning to drag me down. How can I
lift this from my face? Hide it from this young woman

who takes my hand and guides it across the page showing me
the thousand words I have wanted to say to her for so long?

The Journey Begins with the First Step

For Christine

Taking you to the new train station
on this gray day—its stainless angles
of steel against brick and glass—I
talk about almost everything: I
suddenly remember the two a.m. grit
of the old Albany, and I'm sixteen
and waiting in a café for the next bus
to carry me to the Berkshires.

The drunks are all joking loudly
at the counter, and the neon
lateness burns my eyes.
An old man, a lifer from the Navy,
invites me over to crash.
He knows I can't get out
until six.
              So I go to his
place which has only one
bed. I'm not queer, he says,
as he takes off his clothes
down to his boxers.
                       It's a double bed,
and I figure if I keep my clothes on
and lie down way over on my side,
things'll be okay, but he drapes
an arm across my chest
and a leg across my leg . . .

                              I wheel
your suitcase down to the train,
and before you get on,
I look at your golden hair
graying a little like mine.

I want to meet your children,
kick your husband out of bed,

drape myself across you
like that old grubber of a sailor
who only wanted the warmth
of a body beside him—not even love.

Thumbness

I am the extra thumb
the short curve back

to what has been
or never was

I hitch a ride to the might
have been—the will be

I look for the hand
to which you belong

the index finger points
but you . . . turn away

cocking yourself
like a hammer

All the Women I Almost Married

They gather at the edge of a big proscenium like a Greek
chorus keening out their melodious dirges as I prepare
to read my poems to an audience of my peers. They are
not mourning me, nor themselves; instead they mourn
all the women I did marry. Then one of them steps up
whom I think I recognize. She lays her hands upon me
like some blind tent healer, some traveling maiden
all gussied up in a white robe who has laid her hands
for a living every night on a different man
in a different field, outside a different town,
all over the sultry summerscape of America,
and suddenly I hear the whip-o-wills sing as though
I have been blessed by the invisible, the feathers
of something marvelous that passes only once.

Elegy to Socks

The six pairs of running socks you gave me
have all run away as you did.
I shuffle through my drawers
but cannot find them anywhere.

So I write this elegy as if I had
a dozen feet all orphaned and bare.

I think of Neruda, and how little
I know of him, his ode to the socks
he received, their soft rabbit pleasure,
and I think of his stout benefactress
descending from the steep Alpaca places
with her rough peasant hands full
of the billowing wool she would
dye the color of mountain flowers
before she spun and knit her present;

then I imagine their spirits arcing
over the Andes and on through
the breathless lapse of space and time
into this empty drawer I shut now
and walk away from, barefoot as birth.

Red Convertible

For Laura

You call me about your car—*why does it smoke?*
I want to say desire has caught your engine
and your well-oiled heart has frozen from the heat.
—Or should I use the male vocabulary I've heard
around the bottles of beer at cook outs
when the men gather at one end of the table
and the women find themselves at the other
turning over the lumpy potato salads of their lives?

In the end I take the male high road—I
suggest your radiator leaks under pressure.
I too leak under pressure. The hot air puffing
up my chest sighs down like a balloon,
and the hero in me suddenly sees himself
as ordinary as a man who gets on the bus
in the morning and steps off in the evening
knowing nothing but the humdrum of his heart,

hoping for the red convertible of your smile
to pass by and give him a lift.

Portulaca

Portulaca, I said, *Por-tu-lac-a?*
to the young girl at the nursery,
and she smiled, her eyes brightening
from some memory like jewels
turning in a light I couldn't see.

She looked around, then said,
We're sold out,
her eyes taking on another hue.

All around us things flowered
in the misty gray,
red, orange, pink and blue,
as though shouting
against the sunlessness of the day.

Portulaca—a plant I didn't know,
I was just buying for a friend,
when from that old greenhouse
inside me where all the plants
jostled and groped for more dark,
the word suddenly blossomed
burning through almost like a sun,

and for that one moment it hung
between us, a bright talisman,
before the gray air erased it,
and I went home to my friend.

Frame of Reference with Sun Breaking Through

If the truth be known, I lied about the sun: how its
light shafted through the parting clouds as if
an unknown entity were blessing the landscape below,
the curving rows of grain molded to the hill's shape,
how the field dipped out of sight then rose again
from an unseen vale climbing like the pelted back
of some animal yet to be classified: *phylum,
genus, species.*

        Even the landscape I made up
cobbling together parts of Breughel with memories
of a child's book, *The Farmer in the Dell, Old MacDonald,*
the perfect rows of corn corduroying into the horizon,
and somewhere midfield and off-center to the left
a red tractor tries to gain the top of the hill.

Back to the sun:
I could have just left it there,
the high drama of its shafts stabbing
inspiration into the brown and green land,
demonstrating how divine intervention
plays out its not so subtle hand,
and you could have gone home,
rolled down your bed for the night
and pulled up the covers against the dark
knowing that the unconsciousness of sleep
was still safe, and the brush strokes
of my hand were benevolent, as always,

but I have left clouds, instead, and you must
sort through the sky as best you can.

At a Walmart in Southern New Hampshire

What landscape will we never see again
which the imagination has bulldozed into this
commerce, this macadam sea where cars gather
like schooled fish and people enter the blinding
neon of this place as if the sun were darkness?
And you, Walt Whitman, greet me at the door,
naked without your hat, retired old scribbler
with the sun's smile pinned to your blue smock—I'd
recognize your slouch and stubble anywhere.

We walk together down aisles of lawn care
like aging lawn-boys shuffling our bootsoles
toward the certainty of astro turf,
tweaking, along the way, the plastic flowers
in their plastic places, trying to ruffle
the stiff pinkness out of the gay flamingoes
spiked fast to their styrofoam stands. Suddenly,
you turn to me with an old eagle's fierceness
I will remember as much as these words:

Someday, this will all be funky with history,
and a patina of ancient ways and wisdom
will settle over this place to make it all look
like a temple. Tourists will come and fan themselves
leaning against these walls in the hot sun,
and as the day-glo shards of the flamingoes
wink back, they will wonder what our Gods
were like whose molded images on these shelves
our children reach up to like supplicants.

Bright Yellow Stab

Inside: the sun stabs at everything dark; outside:
Sunday splays its legs into August, the late morning
ages along quelling our minds through the afternoon.
Then the kiddie-bears, once pumping hard at the wheels
of their little trinities, stop and look.

                                 For a moment,
all the backyard sprinklers spritz us with rainbows,
and the plastic wading pools toddle alive
with the unbeknownst.

                            Soon, the *foosh*
and belch of the barbecue will swell into the air.
Then comes hot dog time, the mustard of it all,
while the burgers sweat it out on the grill,
and you and I lie hunky-dory in the long chairs:

just fine … until we hear that twitch of cubes rattling
like a cold music we will never know how to sing.

Honey

A few plots over, a mower buzzes in the heat
like a bee working the flowers for its queen.
What does one say at the grave of someone so
important you wouldn't be here except for her
and the choices she couldn't make? How in her life
she had to flee the Old Testament wrath of her father
and leave the garden hive of her innocence. How in your life
you must thank her for the accident of your birth—
what does one say at such a stranger's grave?

I try to whisper a few words. Dry, fine as pollen,
they still catch in my throat. They feel as foreign
as a language I've never spoken, as foreign as here
(where I've never been before) among the bees where
she rests as if waiting for some sweet *yes* I never
said, some offering that life might mean for me
what it never had for her. So I disgorge my sorry
words for all I may have held against her, for all I've
held against the world, then do my dance and leave.

Early Retirement

My son was six and ready to retire,
to gouge his way through sand traps
and roughs right up to his final reward.
So I gave him the root of all leisure
wrapped in a brown 401k
like a celebratory cigar.

Here, put it in your left breast pocket,
I said, *and roll it over once in a while.*

—But why that pocket? he asked
with the eagerness of a big spender—or
maybe he just wanted to light one end
and suck away on the other?

                              Because,
I said, *you're right-handed, and you will
have to cross your heart to reach it.*

The Third Little Pig

They say happiness is an invitation
to your own pig roast. Not since the wolf
stopped breathing heavily at my door
have I had a visitor, an invitation.

I know—I know—pigs are not exactly popular.
And the old sow said there'd be days like this,
sitting by the fire looking through snapshots
of my two brothers' disaster-ridden houses.

Still, you can say construction has been
very, very good to me. It's kept the wolf
at the door from coming inside, although
I sometimes think it would have been better

to be wanted, to have felt his hunger's
hot breath on my neck just once in my life,
to have been consumed by fire—fear—
love—the apocalypse—or even the wolf—

anything—but this comfy boredom
without even a good bedtime story.

The Catamount

To Henri Cole

—but I have seen the catamount, its stealth
turned wary by our baffling human presence.
Every day, through long summer afternoons,
I waited for it in an abandoned field
to descend the far swale in mythic grace,
my piece poised to blurt out its deafening words.
But the days passed without it coming.

So I put away my gun and readied to leave
when suddenly I saw it waft across the road
like a tawny length of ghost, and I drove
to where the pines succored its shadow
and in the umbering light I saw its long
tail twitch its animal unease just once—
then it was gone, driven deep into that place
where memory and faith mingle in the brain
hunting *a clear purpose for existing.*

The Fisherman on the Screen

As I sit here writing, my fingers twitching
at these keys, I want to tweak up on the screen
before me that one poem *as cold and passionate*
as the dawn. Instead, I see him turn to me,
flick his fly back, and smile through the glass:

The trick is in the line. How you cast back, letting
it unfurl behind you—then forward, rolling its
bight and loop so it alights on target, invisible,
kissing the surface right above your fish. How
you want the line's back and forth flight to always
balance all that's ever been behind you—all the
little hooks in your life—with all that will ever be

before you: the fish, the dawn's passionate
vacancy and the verisimilitude of the fly.

Meditation on a Fabled Life

When my grandson was born, suddenly a long race
I'd forgotten I was even running began to slow
inside my bones, and I remembered a family I'd once
been a part of, wearing the scars of belonging,
the tribal marks of their incapacities, and whose legacy
I'd thrown into the blank air when I'd walked out,
years ago, into that cold New York night, denying
all except the dark dependability between the stars,
even the little benedictions of their light.

How could I have known what I know now, as I looked up
at those stars before I stepped down into the dim, druggy,
underground of the subway to take the train to Philly,
then on to the midpoints of my life, one after the other,
always halving the distance toward its finish as if I were
in a sophist's parable where I could never reach what I pursued?

But when I turned the corner into the dead-end of my adulthood,
I discovered, instead, that I lived in a fable where all the characters
were typecast by the speed and shapes of their bodies, the slow,
squat ones armored with love and the fast stretching their long
limbs uncaringly toward something they could easily overcome.
And I began to circle the Fabulist like a dubious beast in his tale.

How I didn't want to remain trapped in that subtext of eternity,
caught between the scattered hare and the methodical tortoise,
sentenced to a life at the speed of rabbit and forced to shed
everything that could weigh me down as I streaked by all
the unread milestones of my life, each toppling as I passed.
So, when the hare, legs snapping with the over confidence
of his own speed, overtook the slow witted tortoise, and then,
went on to sleep, I, too, slept through my whole life dreaming
of some slow, dependable force moving up from behind.

Naming the Emotions

A therapist I once knew used to ask me to
name my emotions. It made me feel like a
taxidermist: stuffing the pelts of rare species,
refilling their deflated and crumpled bodies,
then placing them in the diorama of my mind.
There I could label them for the children who
would come through once a week in unruly groups,
their teachers trying to contain their unfettered
imaginations long enough to gather them
to view my ruffled grouse of astonishment
as it flew above that long-toothed lion of resentment
which stalked the furry, little pachyderm
of my infancy, whose elfin tusks I once believed
could keep at bay all the predators the world
had ever imagined by piercing their hearts
as hearts had never been pierced before.

A Reflective Voice

Before I began beaming
back my reflections,
as if I were a lighthouse
instead of what I am,

I wrote endless parables
that seemed to journey
through stations of the cross,

their sharp details
pushing like intense thorns
into your brow and mine.

Now I write in a visual way
showing the clear words
all at once, not as words
but forms upon a surface,

and I've disappeared
as a mirror does,
appearing only to be
what the mirror shows

and never what it was:

that invisible past writhing up
to this brittle present
which time may one day shatter
into a million starry pieces.

I see you leaning closer
peering at my reflection,
losing sight of what I see
for want of what you can't.

To you,
I must seem bodiless,
a mere echo of the visible,
anything but persona.

Look at these flecks in my iris,
and you will see that special tint,
a little more silver than sepia,

the vision of true poetry

and not that sentimental stuff
peopled by motherly indifference
and the absence of fathers.

Try to imagine: here,
in the vast cadre of all I reflect,
you, also, appear bodiless to me.

Imagine our intimacy
distilled in my glass,

though even here,

the infinitesimal atoms & cells
of our beings can not mingle.

Can we ever get closer?
Or is it that something always harder
than a reluctance to touch

has solidified between us,
and an *ars poetica* frames us
into this mutual speculation?

How will you ever know
that my body, too, is a fragile spell
I cannot break?

And how will I ever know
that you will listen, that you are
what you claim to be—

and not a soft bag of bones
full of heart and spleen,
one that likes a poem or two
and good advice?

Notes:

"Blackberry Poems": Although the canon I mention in this poem is imaginary, I did have three particular poems in mind: Michael Waters' "Among Blackberries," Robert Haas' "Meditations at Lagunitas" and Galway Kinnell's "Blackberry Eating."

"*Flamants Roses*": is French for flamingoes. I lived for a year just north of the *Camargue* which is located in the delta of the Rhone River and is home to Europe's largest wildlife sanctuary and the most important habitat for the Greater Flamingo in Europe.

"The Wild Boy of *Aveyron*": Victor actually learned a vocabulary of about thirty words, but what resonated for me was the very first word he learned and the one which remained the most important to him: *Lait*, the French word for milk. Although Dr. Itard whose persona I assumed in this poem did give up on trying to civilize and educate Victor, he made sure he and his caretaker were both provided for until they died.

"Falling Off in Another Country": *Mobylette* is a French make of motor bicycle.

"The Catamount": In 1966 I experienced in Marlboro, Vermont, what most would call "an unsubstantiated sighting" of a catamount. Even though the animal was considered to be extinct, I stand by it.

"The Fisherman on the Screen": The quotation "as cold and passionate / as the dawn" are the last lines of Yeats' poem "The Fisherman."

About the Author

Tim Mayo holds an ALB, *cum laude*, from Harvard University and an MFA from The Bennington Writing Seminars. Among the awards his poetry has garnered are two International Merit Awards from *Atlanta Review*, finalist in the 2007 *WinningWriters.com* War Poetry Contest and two nominations to the 2008 Best of the Net Anthology, one from *Babel Fruit* and the other from *The Rose and Thorn Literary E-zine*. In 2000 he was a semi-finalist in the "Discovery"/*The Nation* Poetry Contest and has been awarded two fellowships to the Vermont Studio Center's annual Vermont Artist's Week. His chapbook *The Loneliness of Dogs* (Pudding House Publications) was a finalist in the WCDR 2008 Chapbook Challenge in Ontario, Canada. *The Kingdom of Possibilities* (in slightly different incarnations) has been a semi-finalist for the 2009 Brittingham and Pollock Awards, a finalist for the 2007 Main Street Rag Award and lastly, a finalist for 2009 May Swenson Award. He is a former member of the Brattleboro Literary Festival author committee and lives in Brattleboro, Vermont.

Other Recent Titles from Mayapple Press:

Allison Joseph, *Voice: Poems*, 2009
        Paper, 36 pp, $12.95 plus s&h
        ISBN 978-0932412-751
Josie Kearns, *The Theory of Everything*, 2009
        Paper, 86 pp, $14.95 plus s&h
        ISBN 978-0932412-744
Eleanor Lerman, *The Blonde on the Train*, 2009
        Paper, 164 pp, $16.95 plus s&h
        ISBN 978-0932412-737
Sophia Rivkin, *The Valise*, 2008
        Paper, 38 pp, $12.95 plus s&h
        ISBN 978-0932412-720
Alice George, *This Must Be the Place*, 2008
        Paper, 48 pp, $12.95 plus s&h
        ISBN 978-0932412-713
Angela Williams, *Live from the Tiki Lounge*, 2008
        Paper, 48 pp, $12.95 plus s&h
        ISBN 978-0932412-706
Claire Keyes, *The Question of Rapture*, 2008
        Paper, 72 pp, $14.95 plus s&h
        ISBN 978-0932412-690
Judith Kerman and Amee Schmidt, eds., *Greenhouse: The First 5 Years of
the Rustbelt Roethke Writers' Workshop*, 2008
        Paper, 78 pp, $14.95 plus s&h
        ISBN 978-0932412-683
Cati Porter, *Seven Floors Up*, 2008
        Paper, 66 pp, $14.95 plus s&h
        ISBN 978-0932412-676
Rabbi Manes Kogan, *Fables from the Jewish Tradition*, 2008
        Paper, 104 pp, $19.95 plus s&h
        ISBN 978-0932412-669
Joy Gaines-Friedler, *Like Vapor*, 2008
        Paper, 64 pp, $14.95 plus s&h
        ISBN 978-0932412-652
Jane Piirto, *Saunas*, 2008
        Paper, 100 pp, $15.95 plus s&h
        ISBN 978-0932412-645

For a complete catalog of Mayapple Press publications, please visit our website at *www.mayapplepress.com*. Books can be ordered direct from our website with secure on-line payment using PayPal, or by mail (check or money order). Or order through your local bookseller.